I'M TAKING A NAP

By Bil Keane

FAWCETT GOLD MEDAL • NEW YORK

A Fawcett Gold Medal Book
Published by Ballantine Books
Copyright © 1971 by The Register & Tribune Syndicate, Inc.

All rights reserved under International and Pan-American Copyright Conventions, including the right to reproduce this book or portions thereof in any form. Published in the United States by Ballantine Books, a division of Random House, Inc., New York, and simultaneously in Canada by Random House of Canada Limited, Toronto.

ISBN 0-449-12846-6

This edition published by arrangement with
The Register & Tribune Syndicate, Inc.

Printed in Canada

First Fawcett Gold Medal Edition: February 1974
First Ballantine Books Edition: January 1984
Twenty-fifth Printing: August 1992

"Oh, that's right––I forgot. Daddy called while you were out and he wants you to pick him up at the office."

"It's called 'dominoes'. Want us to show you
how to play it?"

"I woked up very sad this morning 'cause I don't
'member anybody kissing me good
night last night."

"Can I kick it for you this time, Daddy?"

"Stop copying me, PJ!"

"Mommy! Tell Dolly to stop showing everybody her new pants!"

"Lick your fork, Mr. Horton --we're havin' pie for dessert."

"Mommy's lucky! She gets to play in all those bubbles!"

"I'm all out of smiles for today, Daddy."

"But if you put them in the laundry, I won't have
anything to wear!"

"MY hands are CLEAN!"

"Do you have a hanky, Daddy? I couldn't
reach the paper towels."

"Know why I'm lookin' at you, Dolly? I'm trying
to scare myself out of hiccups."

"Can you reach up there for me, Daddy? You're
a little higher than me."

"Is it okay if we get wet, Mommy?"

"I'll have a hamburger, a milk shake and french fries!"

"Why did you write your shopping list on the back of the picture I drew for my teacher?"

"As soon as my hands grow up I'll be able to play cards better."

"You said we'd put up the new bird house today!"

"I told my class I was havin' a birthday party next week. Could I, Mommy?"

"Address one for Donna. She's my best friend."
"What's her last name?"
"I don't know."

"Instead of putting R.S.V.P. if regretting why not just say 'Let us know if you can't come'?"

"I don't know if any of the kids are coming to my party. When I gave them the invitations all they said was 'goody!'"

"Aren't you wearing a party dress, Mommy, like
you do for the grown-up parties?"

"Happy Birthday -- it's a nurse's kit!"

"Mommy, Jeffy's not singing."

"Won't GOD be surprised!"

"Don't worry, PJ, Mommy will SEW it up."

"Thank you for the very pretty five dollar bill,
Grandma...and for the card, too."

"Grandma said I could use the five dollars she gave me to buy ANYTHING I WANTED."

"Bye-bye, PJ...Goodbye, dear...PJ?...
Bye-bye..."

"We didn't take that test today, but that's okay.
At least I got all my pencils sharpened."

"PJ go bye-bye."

"All right, all right -- I'll put you back so you can climb over ALL BY YOURSELF."

"How do you make that excited mark that comes
at the end of a sentence?"

"I forget what I'm lookin' for, Mommy. Can you help me remember?"

"I want a SHINY penny like you gave Billy."

"What part of your face hasn't been kissed yet?"

"Let's see -- there's quinine water, club soda,
lime juice, collins mix, tomato juice..."

"WAIT! We didn't say Grace!"

"When you said Daddy was getting glasses,
I thought you meant the kind
we drink out of."

"Can you see me through your WINDOWS?"

"Now that Daddy's wearing glasses he doesn't look like ME any more."

"What I liked best about school this year was the teachers' strike."

"Daddy! You forgot 'em again!"

"Scott's LUCKY! He only has to wash
ONE hand."

"Oh, oh! It's raining and it put the stars out."

"Mommy, will you tell Jeffy to stop it? He's
singing at the wrong speed."

"When the lady said 'this is a recording' I said
'thank you' but she didn't say
'you're welcome!'"

"Wowee! THIS one's REALLY old! It was born the same year as Daddy."

"Having PJ around the house is almost as good as having another pet."

"Can I try out my new bathing suit in the bathtub?"

"Darn you, PJ! You scared him away!"

"It's very warm tonight so I don't think I'll wear my covers."

"He's okay, Mommy--he's not doing anything.
He's just going through that old book
Mrs. Bombeck lent you."

"Daddy always gives us each a WHOLE one
without splittin' it."

"I gave that plant a drink of water. Do you
hear it swallowing?"

"If we're going to Mr. Kelly's farm we better pack some TOOLS!"

"You guys HAVE to stay at the vet's while we're on vacation. Daddy only got plane tickets for the TWO LEGGED people in the family."

"There goes a plane! I know it's ours and we MISSED it!"

"Destination, Sir?   "Mr. Kelly's farm!"

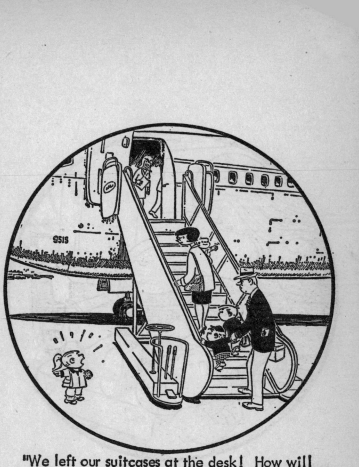

"We left our suitcases at the desk! How will
they know which plane we got on?"

"No, this isn't my first plane ride. I was on the
WHIRL-O-PLANE once at Kiddie Park."

"Stop leanin' over here, Jeffy--you'll make
the plane TILT!"

"We're going to the little boys' room...We're
going to the little boys' room...We're
going to the..."

"I wish this food would float all around the
cabin like it does for the astronauts."

"PJ's doing nothin' but sleeping -- he's missing
all the scenery!"

"Daddy, if you're scared while we're landing
you can hold onto my hand."

"I didn't get to sit by the window!"

"My word of honor, Peg -- we're only staying a WEEK!"

"Hang on, everybody --we'll be there in an hour."

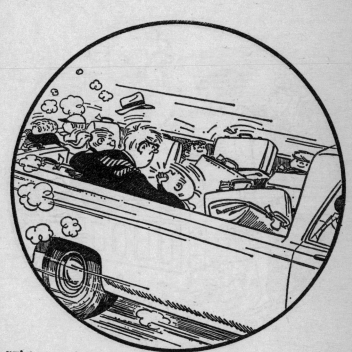

"This is a lot better than RENTING A CAR, isn't it, Daddy?"

"Jeffy won't get out -- he's afraid of
the chickens."

"I wish we could sleep in the hay in that barn."

"Us farmers don't need an alarm clock -- we'll
wake up when we hear the rooster yell."

"...This little pig had roast beef, this little pig
had none..."

"I want to sit on the tractor."

"Why do the Kellys say we're havin' DINNER
when it's just LUNCHTIME?"

"Gee, that chicken sure wiped her feet clean
before she went in the house!"

"Okay, cool it, rooster! We're UP!"

"S'posing the 'lectricity goes off -- THEN how
can you get the milk?"

"What are their names?"

"This air smells funny -- I guess it doesn't have
enough PLUTION. in it."

"MOMMY!"

"Please, Mommy? Can we take him home with us? He could sleep in my room and I'LL take care of him."

"G'bye, chickens! G'bye, cows! G'bye, horses! G'bye, sheep! G'bye, pigs! G'bye, ducks! G'bye..."

"NOW how many miles have we gone, Daddy?"

"I had a nice time, my lunch was delicious and
tell the pilot that was a very good landing."

"I'll find it, Daddy! It's the one with PJ's teddy bear on the back seat."

"After looking at the horses and cows and those other animals on the farm, don't Barfy and Sam look LITTLE?"

"We had a real OLD FASHIONED vacation on a FARM--we flew there in a 727."

"I shooted you, Billy!   "You missed me."
C'mon--play dead."

"I hope I don't get skinned-up knees. I'm going
to try to fall on my bottom every time."

"It's Billy's fault 'cause he's the oldest and he should know better!"

"PJ picked that up from Kittycat. It means
he's hungry."

"We had a substitute today, but she was just like a REAL teacher. She knew how to yell and everything!"

"Stop it, Billy! I wanna get off!"

"I wasn't REALLY scared. I was just be-tending."

"It's okay --I didn't get any on the tablecloth."

"I'm for the yellow guys, Daddy--who are you
voting for?"
"The Blue Guys."
"Me, too."

"Go·'way, PJ! I'm not just sitting here having fun! This is my HOMEWORK!"

"Miss Johnson would give you a C in writing,
Daddy. She's an easy marker."

"Shouldn't you wait 'til Daddy gets home? It says 'MR. AND MRS.'"

"Can I ride home with the O'Connors? They
always stop for ice cream."

"I learned some Spanish! Listen: SI!"

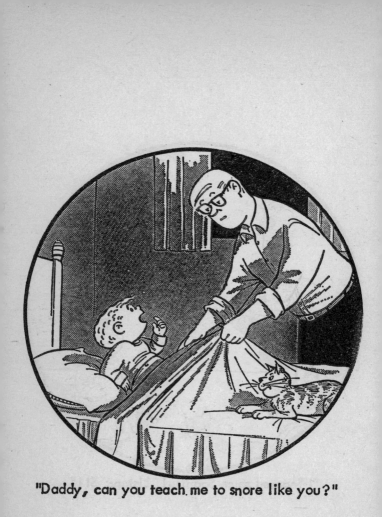

"Daddy, can you teach me to snore like you?"

"Some lady called to see if you would collect on
this block for something. I said you would."

"Rain is GOOD! It gives the flowers a drink,
washes the driveway and we can watch TV."

"I played so hard today I got almost as dirty as a boy!"

"Can I turn on television, Mommy? Kitty-cat
wants to keep warm."

"Would you believe that's not catchup or jelly
but a REAL HURT?"

"Thank you, door!"

"Know what somebody did? Somebody hid their
crusts under their plate."

"Are my socks on the right feet?"

"Let ME whack her, Mommy! Let ME!"

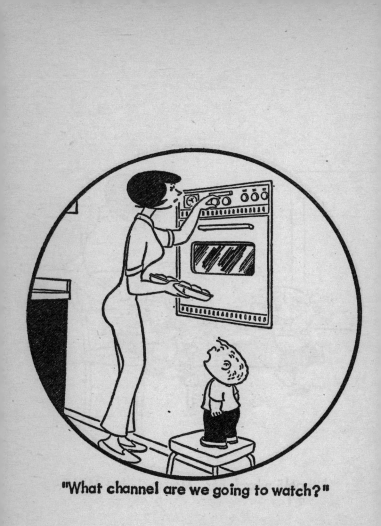

"What channel are we going to watch?"

"This book Grandma sent me is very good. So far I can only read the pictures but it's very good."

"I have to practice my lines for the play. They're 'GOBBLE, GOBBLE'."

"...And for all these things we are thankful,
Amen. Now, for Christmas I want a
bake set, a doll crib, a..."

"I'm going to work this wishbone all by myself
'cause then maybe I'll win for a change."

"Mommy! PJ's drinking all the water and we're
not finished taking our bath in it yet!"

"Aw -- I TOLD the frog to stay here while I
got you."

"Daddy, how many facts of life are there?"